WHY

in THE WORLD
WOULD YOU

CHOOSE

TO GO TO

HELL?

WHY

in THE WORLD WOULD YOU

CHOOSE
TO GO TO

HELL?

The Real 'Choice'

R. STEPHEN MICHAEL

WHY IN THE WORLD WOULD YOU CHOOSE TO GO TO HELL? THE REAL 'CHOICE'

iUniverse books may be ordered through booksellers or by contacting:

iUniverse
1663 Liberty Drive
Bloomington, IN 47403
www.iuniverse.com
844-349-9409

Because of the dynamic nature of the Internet, any web addresses or links contained in this book may have changed since publication and may no longer be valid. The views expressed in this work are solely those of the author and do not necessarily reflect the views of the publisher, and the publisher hereby disclaims any responsibility for them.

Any people depicted in stock imagery provided by Getty Images are models, and such images are being used for illustrative purposes only.
Certain stock imagery © Getty Images.

Scriptures taken from the New King James Version. ©1982 by Thomas Nelson. Used by permission. All rights reserved.

ISBN: 978-1-6632-3723-1 (sc)
ISBN: 978-1-6632-3722-4 (e)

Library of Congress Control Number: 2022904905

Print information available on the last page.

iUniverse rev. date: 03/21/2022

CONTENTS

PREFACE

The world we live in today changes at a frantic pace.

The internet has brought about an explosion of information. It provides an opportunity to unite the world, and at the same time an opportunity to distance people. But one thing never changes. At some point in every life, death will present itself. How we view death will depend on how we chose to live.

Communism with its desire for domination has again risen its ugly head. Russia's invasion of Ukraine is an effort to take over Ukraine to reestablish and expand the old Soviet Union. China is watching the world's reaction to the Russian invasion as it contemplates taking over Taiwan and has announced its intention to rule the entire South China Sea. Iran is speeding toward nuclear weapons to destroy Israel and threaten the United States. Radical Islam is trying to bring about international chaos and destruction to hasten the coming of their messiah. Covid-19 has totally rearranged the way the world around us operates. These things have brought great fear into people's minds.

For thousands of years, people have believed that God exists and created everything. But now the world, and sadly even the United States, have turned on God, denying in many cases that He even exists. We have removed Him from schools, government and daily life because He and His rules are inconvenient. The result is chaos, lawlessness and crime, and broken lives.

For thousands of years the Bible was respected as God's word. Now it's often called racist or hate speech. The Bible tells us that there is an afterlife with two possible eternal (forever) destinations. One is eternal happiness in a place called heaven. The other is eternal torture in a place called hell. Where you go is a choice you, and only you, must make.

My late wife was a Bible scholar, fluent in Greek and Hebrew. We spent many hours studying the Bible and her text books as she worked on her Bachelor's in Christian Religion and Philosophy. She started working on her master's degree in Biblical Studies but was stricken with Parkinson's disease and never got the masters degree. But she kept on studying on her own and passed much of the knowledge she acquired on to me. She wanted to teach Biblical Studies at the seminary level, but never got the chance. So, it's up to me to pass the knowledge along in this book.

I write this book in the hope of informing you how to make the choice for heaven and not hell. It is far and away the most important decision you will ever make.

Don't wait. Do it now!

CHAPTER

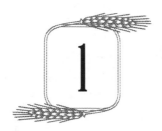

My Soul, My Choice

Why in the world would you choose to go to hell?

Ever thought about that question? Ever realized that you do choose to go there? You're probably saying, "That's crazy—nobody would choose to go to hell!" Well, unless you've made a conscious decision to go to heaven, you've chosen to go to hell. Why? Because when we are born, we are all under the stain of Adam's sin and destined for hell. That's why Jesus said in John 3:18,

> He who believes in Him is not condemned; but he
> who does not believe is condemned already; because
> he has not believed in the name of the only begotten
> Son of God.

If you get nothing else from this book, please get this: making a choice is not optional. Do nothing, and you'll end up in hell forever. Not making the choice to accept God's plan of salvation in Jesus, having your sins forgiven and repenting of them, *is* making the choice to go to hell! St. Paul wrote in his letter to the Romans, "For the wages of sin is death [hell], but the gift of God is life [heaven] in Christ Jesus our Lord." (Romans 6:23) It is not either/or; "Oh, I can make a choice or not." If you don't make a choice for heaven, you won't be there. [Emphasis mine.]

If you have ever watched the evening or late-night news, you've probably seen marches in favor of abortion. Woman carry signs saying: My Body My Choice. They, and for that matter all of us, should carry signs reading: 'My Soul My Choice'. Decisions we make here on earth determine where we will spend eternity.

But let's start at the beginning.

As children we should have been taught about God, heaven and hell, and the Bible (which is God's Word written down) by our parents or at church. The different churches had training books called catechisms. These catechisms often start with three simple questions and answers.

Who made me?
God made me.

Who is God?
God is the creator of everything. (We'll explore this in depth in chapter 2.)

Why did God make me?
To know, love, and serve Him in this life so we can be with Him in heaven in the next.

God is a spirit. Merriam-Webster online dictionary defines *God* as: the Being perfect in power, wisdom and goodness who is worshipped (as in Judaism, Christianity, Islam and Hinduism) as the creator and ruler of the universe. Interestingly, a second definition is: a being or object that is worshipped as having more than natural attributes and powers. The second definition will have more meaning later.

God lives in a place called heaven. No one knows where heaven is or what it really is. God tells us that it is a place of perfect love, peace, and happiness. We also know that it is not on earth!

Oh, you don't believe in God? That's strange, because the devil from hell knows God and definitely believes in Him. In Genesis 3:1 the serpent (Satan) approaches Eve and asks her: "Has God indeed said, 'You shall not eat of every tree in the garden'?" No hesitation or question about the existence of God, just questioning and twisting His command. Not only does Satan believe in God, he interacts with Him. Job 1:6–7 says:

> Now there was a day when the sons of God came to present themselves before the Lord, and Satan also came among them. And the Lord said to Satan: "From where do you come?" So, Satan answered the Lord and said, "From going to and fro on the earth, and walking back and forth on it."

And what do you think Satan was doing on earth? Well, 1 Peter 5:8 tells us he was "walking about like a roaring lion, seeking whom he may devour." In other words, he was looking for souls to lead to hell.

I know, you don't believe in the Bible either. Well, Satan believes in it and quotes it when it is to his advantage. Matthew 4:5–6 tells us that when Jesus had been in the desert for forty days fasting and praying, Satan came to Him and used words from Psalms to tempt Him.

> He took Him up in the holy city, set Him on the pinnacle of the temple and said to Him: "If you are the Son of God, throw Yourself down. For it is written: 'For He shall give His angels charge over you to keep you in all your ways' and 'In their hands they shall bear you up, lest you dash your foot against a stone.'"

If Satan knows and quotes the Bible (specifically, Psalm 91:11–12) and interacts with God, and he can never go back to heaven, why wouldn't you do the same, since you can go to heaven?

A long time ago, God created beings called angels. Merriam–Webster online defines an angel as a spiritual being serving as a divine messenger and intermediary and often as a special protector of a person or nation. Like the army, the angels in heaven have ranks. The highest rank are the archangels, who stand next to God himself. We know of four by name: Michael, Gabriel, Raphael, and Lucifer. Lucifer rebelled against God. He led a rebellion, and a third of heaven's angels followed him (Rev. 12:4). "His tail drew a third of the stars of heaven and threw them to the earth." [This passage of scriptures has been interpreted to mean the angels that followed Satan in his rebellion.] They were defeated by Michael and the rest of heaven's angels and were thrown out of heaven into a place God created just for them, called hell. Hell is a place of punishment for the wicked. Hell was not created, nor meant, for people. Lucifer became Satan, the devil, and the angels that followed him are called demons.

Then came man.

But let's look at where we live. We live on a planet called Earth which revolves around a star we call the sun. Other planets revolve around the sun to form what we call the solar system. Our sun is one of millions of stars in a galaxy called the Milky Way. The Milky Way is one of millions of galaxies in a space called the universe.

The first book of the Bible is Genesis. Genesis 1:1 tells us that "in the beginning, God created the heavens and the earth." In Genesis 1:3, "God said, 'Let there be light' and there was light." In other words, God spoke everything into existence. He created space, and all the stars and planets, out of nothing. That includes us. He created a man by taking dirt from the earth and molding it and breathed life into the man and put him in a place called the Garden of Eden. He saw that the man was lonely so He created a mate for the man, who is called woman. They lived together, and God visited with them in the garden.

When God put the man and woman in the garden, He told them not to eat the fruit of the tree in the middle of the garden or they would die. Unfortunately, Satan, the devil, told the woman Eve that God had lied to them, and she believed it. They disobeyed God and ate the fruit. So He had to throw them out of the garden, and they had to work the soil for their food. This is the basic story of Creation as told by God in the Bible.

Unfortunately, progressive modern science teaches that everything just evolved on its own after what scientists call the 'big bang.' It teaches that there is no God and that everything happened in a process called evolution. If you look at the universe as a whole as just evolving in random happenstance, you could possibly develop a workable theory. But upon closer examination, the universe displays an order and detail that could never have just evolved.

For example, the earth is 93 million miles from the sun. This, it turns out, is the perfect distance from the sun for a planet to support life. Any closer and the sun's heat would make life impossible, as on Venus. Any further out and while life could have started, the distance from the sun would allow the planet's core to cool, eventually denying the planet of its protective magnetic field. The lack of the magnetic field's protection would allow the solar wind to strip the planet of its atmosphere, killing the planet's ability to support life. Scientists now believe that happened on Mars. Is it just happenstance that earth is the perfect distance?

Before we go on, we need to define and explain a black hole. Stars eventually burn up all their fuel and burn out or die. When huge stars, three times or more the size of our sun, die or burn out, they collapse in on themselves and sometimes create a hole in space. Because they were so big, they have a great gravity that stays with them after they die. This gravity causes them to pull in matter and energy from the area around them. Light cannot escape from them, and thus the name black hole.

Now let's look at the big bang theory. Where did the energy and matter that made up the big bang come from? When Steven Hawking did his major work on black holes, he hypothesized that at some point in its history, conditions inside the black hole make it volatile enough to explode. Some scientists again hypothesize that this is what the big bang was. If that's the case, there had to be another universe where the black hole resided for the energy and matter to come from. While one *might* believe happenstance, or chance, caused one universe to develop, it really strains belief to stretch it to two or more universes.

Also, if a black hole can explode, what keeps it from exploding back into the universe it came from? For it not to explode back into the universe it resided in, it has to explode out the back or side of the hole and create a rip in the fabric of space/time, which creates a whole new universe, like ours. Why wouldn't it explode back out into the universe it came from? Is the gravitational pull greater than the strength of the fabric of space/time? And who determined that?

Imagine for a second a black hole did explode back into the universe in which it resided. The sudden inrush of matter and energy would disrupt the entire order of the universe and blow galaxies and solar systems apart. What would that do to life as we know it? What random pattern of evolution prevents this from happening? Nothing! It takes a superior mind to bring the kind of forethought and knowledge of what could happen if the universe were left to its own devices into the design of the universe. That mind belongs to the being we call God. He created it and designed it to maintain the order He established in it from the beginning.

Could the big bang actually account for the beginning of our universe? Of course it could! If He *told* a black hole to explode and create another universe, it would be done. After all the Bible does say He *spoke* everything into existence. And wouldn't an explosion bring light? Think for a second how fantastic a mind He must have to design and control our universe, and all the universes that could have been created by this process. Wouldn't you want to get to know Him and be with Him forever?

I am not under any circumstances trying to discredit the biblical story of Creation, nor am I saying that man evolved, as Darwin did. But the evidence is there that this universe is billions of years old and still is in the process of creation to this day. Nebulae, gas clouds millions of light years big, are nurseries where new stars are being born today. These new stars can then create new galaxies and the universe grows. God spoke it into existence and set the process into motion for the creation of an expanding, growing universe, and even possibly more universes at His word. And that process is still in motion today, because He enjoys creating and guiding all of His creation.

I know there will be some in the church that will say this thinking is absurd or even heretical. Why? Do you serve the small "i am" or the great "I AM"? God is limitless in His power and abilities. Why do we put Him in a box because He wrote the Genesis creation story in a way that our finite minds could understand and so believe that He is the Creator? Bill Crowder, writing in Our Daily Bread monthly devotional, put it more eloquently than I ever could: "Our God is too great, vast, and incomprehensible to be minimalized or neatly packaged. His ways and thoughts are beyond us, which means that we in our finiteness must learn to accept the mysteries of His greatness."[1]

"O Lord my God, when I in awesome wonder consider all the worlds Thy hands have made": we hear these words from "How Great Thou Art" on the radio or sing them in church, but do we really believe them? Or if we believe, do we ever contemplate the implications? You probably don't want to hear it, but God doesn't live in the box we put Him in in our minds. We create an image of God to fit what we want Him to be instead of who He is. Because we cannot fathom His infinity, we limit Him to what we can understand and create a false God.

The church excommunicated Galileo when he said that the earth was not the center of the solar system and that everything did not revolve around the earth. The sun is the center of our solar system, as Galileo predicted.

God is not a doddering, bearded, gray-haired old man sitting on a throne in heaven, as we often see Him pictured, who was tired out after creating the first universe. As Isaiah 40:28 tells us, "The Creator of the ends of the earth neither faints nor is weary. His understanding is unsearchable." God is an all-powerful spirit who is still at work today. The problem comes from the intersection of a rigid interpretation of the Genesis story of creation colliding with what we know from science about the time it has taken for this universe to arrive at its present state. If we remember that God is always in the present—and 2 Peter 3:8 tells us "with the Lord one day is as a thousand years, and a thousand years as one day"—then there doesn't have to be any conflict between the Bible and science regarding Creation versus evolution.

---

[1]   Taken from Our Daily Bread ® ©2020 Our Daily Bread Ministries, Grand Rapids, MI. Reprinted by permission. All rights reserved.

After the earth cooled, God created all life, animate and inanimate, including huge creatures known as dinosaurs. In His time, He commanded a meteor to strike the earth and create an atmosphere toxic to life, killing off the dinosaurs. When the atmosphere recovered millions of years ago, He created a garden which flourished and became the centerpiece of the earth. There He created his masterpiece, man and woman, placed them in the garden and gave them authority over all the living things on earth. But man sinned against God and was thrown out of the garden.

More importantly, before God ever created anything, He knew everything. Did you ever stop to think that before He created man, He knew that Adam and Eve were going to sin against Him? And yet the Bible says that He looked at His creation and saw that it was good. How is that? Well, since He knew beforehand, He already had His plan of salvation ready before He created anything.

In the Garden of Eden, just after Adam had sinned, God told the Satan disguised as a serpent, "And I will put enmity between you and the woman. And between your seed and her seed; He shall bruise your head, and you shall bruise His heel" (Genesis 3:14). God promised in the garden that He would send the offspring of the woman to redeem man from his sin and reopen the gates of heaven. That promise was carried through the ages in the prophecies and belief that the redeemer, or Messiah, would come to redeem mankind and reestablish the relationship with God as it was at the beginning. Jesus of Nazareth was the predicted offspring of the woman that God talked about, and He crushed Satan's head on the cross, after Satan struck at His heel by causing others to condemn Him to death on the cross.

Some may remember Rainbow Man, as he came to be known, at sporting events in the 1970s and 1980s with his little John 3:16 sign. Well, unfortunately, Rainbow Man actually did the world a disservice by not telling the whole message. You see, in John 3:16 Jesus told Nicodemus: "For God so loved the world that He gave His only begotten Son, that whoever who believes in Him should not perish but have everlasting life." Verse 17 continues, "For God did not send His Son into the world to condemn the world, but that the world through Him might be saved." Maybe we are ashamed of what we have done and don't want to disclose it to God. He already knows! He knew you were going to do it before you were ever born. He's just waiting for you to confess it to Him and accept His forgiveness.

In John 8:3-11 we read the story of a woman caught in adultery:

> Then the scribes and Pharisees brought to Him a woman caught in adultery. And when they had set her in the midst, they said to Him, "Teacher, this woman was caught in adultery, in the very act. Now Moses, in the law, commanded us that she should be stoned. But what do you say?" This they said, testing Him, that they might have something of which to accuse Him. But Jesus stooped down and wrote on the ground with His finger, as though He did not hear. So when they continued asking Him, He raised Himself up and said to them, "He who is without sin among you, let him throw a stone at her first." And again He stooped down and wrote on the ground. Those who heard it, being convicted by their conscience, went one by one, beginning with the eldest even to the last. And Jesus was left alone, and the woman standing in the midst. When Jesus had raised Himself up and saw no one but the woman, He said to her, "Woman, where are those accusers of yours? Has no one condemned you?" She said, "No one, Lord." And Jesus said to her, "Neither do I condemn you; go and sin no more."

But Jesus added very emphatically in John 3:18, "He who believes in Him is not condemned; but whoever refuses to believe is already condemned, because he has not believed in the name of the only begotten Son of God". Why would He say that? Remember the sin of Adam—believing is the choice of heaven.

You hear people today say, "A truly loving God would never condemn anyone to hell." They are correct. God never condemned anyone to hell. We condemn ourselves by not believing in Jesus, God's only plan of salvation. We condemn ourselves by not accepting the salvation offered by believing in Jesus and giving our lives to Him. Believe it or not, getting to heaven is just that simple. Religion tries to complicate it with rituals and physical rules, but the reality is that believing in Jesus, accepting His gift of salvation, and following God's Word is all that is required.

The world laughs at believing in Jesus and the Bible. Many are afraid to embrace Christianity because they don't want to be laughed at. But there is an old expression: "He who laughs last, laughs loudest." Who's laughing? Not Christians. They cry as God does for the souls being lost. So, who's laughing? Satan, the devil from hell! He's laughing his ass off because he knows the condition of the souls of those who fail to believe and where they are headed. He's got them just where he wants them because they believe his lies.

Whom do you want laughing at you? The world, now, on a temporary basis? Or Satan, forever?

God said: "I call on heaven and earth as witnesses today against you, that I have set before you life and death, blessing and cursing; therefore, choose life, that both you and your descendants may live" (Deuteronomy 30:19). That means He gives each of us free will to choose Him and heaven, or the devil and hell. Because he said it, He has to honor whatever choice we make. If we choose to follow the devil and to go to hell, He has to send us there. But it is *our* choice, not His.

Imagine the fantastic risk He took in giving us free will. He loves each of us so much and wants each of us in heaven with Him forever. He could have eliminated that risk by making us like puppets on a string, doing everything He commanded us to do, thus guaranteeing that we would be in heaven. But He didn't want puppets. He wanted people who would choose Him and return the great love He has for us and want to be with Him in heaven.

So why don't people want to choose life and God? Because we get caught up in the world and all that it offers and don't want to give it up. But who said you have to give it up? In Mathew 6:33, Jesus said, "Seek first the kingdom of God and His righteousness, and all these things will be added unto you." He never said that you have to give everything up. On the contrary, God promised that He would give us what we need, and more, if we put Him first in our lives and follow Him.

In Matthew 16:26, Jesus said: "For what profit is it to a man if he gains the whole world and loses his own soul? Or what will a man give in exchange for his soul?" What money, power, sex, or possessions could make going through torment forever, instead of enjoying peace and eternal love in heaven, worth it? I know I could never come up with anything that made enough sense to justify that kind of decision.

Imagine for a moment you're on death row in prison. The governor writes a pardon and has it delivered to the warden. They bring it to you and tell you that you are to be freed. Would you turn down the pardon? I don't think so! Well, we are all born on spiritual death row for eternity because of Adam's sin in the garden. Jesus is the pardon God has given us. Why would you fail to accept it by not believing in Him?

The church has for centuries tried to figure out what the "unpardonable sin" is that Jesus talked about. It's very simple: failing to ask for forgiveness and accepting God's only plan of salvation in Jesus, His Son. If we don't acknowledge our sin and ask for forgiveness, we can't be forgiven. That makes it unpardonable not to ask!

People often describe a horrific experience as "hell on earth." There can never be such a thing, no matter how horrible the circumstances. As long as you are alive on the earth you have hope of contacting God, establishing a relationship with Him, and accepting His plan of salvation. But once you die and leave this world, all hope of that is gone. It's too late!

CHAPTER

WHO IS GOD?

It would be presumptuous or maybe even blasphemous for a human being to say that they know who God is and can describe or explain Him. Our finite minds cannot begin to comprehend such an infinite being. But, like any loving parent, God gave us a way to get to know Him and begin to comprehend a little of who and what He is. That way is His Living Word, His Son, who was on the earth as the man Jesus of Nazareth. Through the inspiration of God's Spirit, man has written down this way in the Bible. Starting with Genesis and all the way to Revelation, we see God at work, revealing Jesus and Himself to us.

But first, let us look at the name God. Merriam-Webster defines *name* as: name or phrase that constitutes the distinctive designation of a person or thing is called. Everything and everyone have a name. It is the way we identify and distinguish persons and things. By itself, a name only gives information about identity but does not lead to knowledge. Knowledge comes from researching and studying the person or thing. Every language and culture call Him something different. Native

...ericans call Him the Great Spirit. Jewish people call Him by many ...ames, including Yahweh, Jehovah, El Shaddai, and Elohim. Muslims call Him Allah.

"God" is just a word or name that most people have heard of. It carries no meaning for the hearer until we gain knowledge of who and what He is. But we can only know Him by His revelation of His attributes.

In Exodus 34:6–7, we see God revealing something of Himself as He describes some of His attributes to Moses:

> And the Lord passed before him and proclaimed. "The Lord, the Lord God, merciful and gracious, longsuffering, and abounding in goodness and truth, keeping mercy for thousands, forgiving iniquity and transgression and sin, by no means clearing the guilty, visiting the iniquity of the fathers upon the children and the children's children to the third and fourth generation.

Let's explore some of these and other of His attributes.

1. **God is merciful and gracious.** Roman 5:8–11 says God loves every individual so much that He demonstrates His own love toward us, in that while we were still sinners, Christ died for us. Much more then, having been justified by His blood, we shall be saved from wrath through Him. For if when we were enemies we were reconciled to God through the death of His Son, much more, having been reconciled, we shall be saved by His life. And not only that, but we also rejoice in God through our Lord Jesus Christ, through whom we have now received the reconciliation.

When man sinned against Him, He could have abandoned us to the devil. He didn't because of His love and graciousness. Instead, He reached out to us and offered us a way of salvation. If God had created only one person on earth, and that person was you, He still would have

sent Jesus to die for you to be reconciled to Him and lead you to heav
How can you turn your back on that kind of mercy and love?

2. **God is long-suffering.** "Long-suffering" describes one who exhibits long and patient endurance of offenses. God forgives us even when we repeatedly sin against Him, even with the same sin. Matthew 18:21–22 tells us:

> Then Peter came to Him and said, "Lord, how often shall my brother sin against me, and I forgive him? Up to seven times?" Jesus said to him, "I do not say to you up to seven times, but seventy times seven."

If Jesus tells us to forgive seventy times seven times, how much more will a patient, loving God forgive us when we sin against Him? But be careful! Patience, even God's, does have a point of no return. Long-suffering and forgiveness demand repentance and changing your ways as well.

3. **God is Spirit.** Exactly what that means is a mystery. But unlike us, God has no physical body. When He said, "Let us make man in our own image," He was referring to the spiritual realm, not the physical. He has revealed that He is a being of three distinct persons in one God: Father, Son and Holy Spirit (which is called the Trinity). He created man and woman to be united together with Him in a union (marriage) which mirrors the Trinity. That is the image of God He was talking about.

It's in the soul, or spirit, united with God, that we are in His image. Did you ever stop to think that before Eve was created, there is no record in the Bible that Satan ever bothered Adam? It was only after Eve was created and placed with Adam that the image of the Trinity was on earth in the three-way union. Satan couldn't abide that, so he had to attack man and destroy this relationship. He wanted control over man on the earth, and unfortunately Adam gave it to him.

Many people today mistakenly believe that there is a war going on in heaven between God and Satan. Some actually believe that Satan

...ld win. Nothing could be further from the truth. Satan was defeated
...n heaven by Michael, the archangel, and the forces of heaven eons ago
and forced from heaven into a region created by God specially for him
and his followers, called hell. Luke 10:18 tells us, And He said to them,
"I saw Satan fall like lightning from heaven." The only battle here on
earth is in the spiritual realm: Satan's war against the souls of people to
get them to choose to follow him to hell.

God created one race when He created man: the human race.
As people migrated from the original place of creation, geographical
differences caused genetic mutations or variations in four chromosomes,
out of forty-six chromosomes in our cells. These variations caused the
differences in people's looks. Man was created as one race, the human
race, by God. All are equal in God's eyes. White supremacists or other
hate groups who think they are the ones who look most like God, and
thus are superior, are in for a rude awakening when they finally meet
God in judgment.

4. **God is Creator.** Genesis 1:1, "In the beginning, God created
   the heavens and the earth." He took nothing and turned it into
   a beautiful universe. He did it by His Word. Genesis 1:3, "Then
   God said: 'Let there be light'; and there was light." What process or
   length of time He used is not important. The fact is that at His Word
   it happened, in the manner and with the outcome that He wanted.
   As discussed earlier, whether He created one universe or started a
   process in motion which has produced millions of universes, we
   know that He is the creator.

And we know that He is proud of His creation. He revels in showing
it off by allowing us to slowly gain an understanding of it. Think about
it for a second: in 1920, just one hundred years ago, we knew nothing
of quasars, pulsars, black holes, or nebulae. Airplanes were stick-and-
fabric single-seat fighters which had become operational in World
War I. Electrifying homes was beginning to be standard. Radio was
in its infancy, and there wasn't any television. We knew nothing of
x-rays, Doppler shift, dark matter, and energy, and could hardly look
beyond our own solar system into the Milky Way galaxy. Today we use

powerful space telescopes to study galaxies billions of light-years distant and take pictures of black holes. Multi-engine jets carry people all over the globe. We've landed men on the moon, and people permanently orbit the earth in a space station. Microwaves cook our food and send signals around the world on cell phones. He has given us more and more knowledge as we have been able to absorb it.

Unfortunately, this knowledge has often driven man farther from God instead of drawing Him closer. Scientists look for explanations in the physical world instead of in the spiritual world and lead people astray. Darwin speculated that the universe and the world are evolving, but drew the wrong conclusions on how, by excluding God from the process.

Many in the church argue against theistic evolution, the view that God drives the evolving process in His time and way. But as we gain more knowledge of the universe, it is obvious that it is still growing and as such is evolving. Nothing happens in the universe or on this earth without His knowledge and consent. That statement could lead some to question why He allows the disasters and hardships that befall people all the time. But we have to remember that we have free will and often set ourselves up for the situations that befall us. And as St. Paul wrote in Romans 8:22, "For we know the whole creation groans and labors with birth pangs together until now." Because of man's sin, natural disasters, storms, plagues, and the like are products of an earth that groans, awaiting its salvation.

Some might argue that statement elevates man's importance too high. But we have to remember that God created the earth as the home of man and gave him dominion over it. Man gave that dominion away when he sinned. Satan gained influence over the earth, and it has suffered for it ever since.

5. **God is love.** In the 1960s, Steve McQueen starred in a TV show called *Wanted Dead or Alive*. The show opened with bounty hunter McQueen walking up to a wall and tearing down a wanted poster of a criminal. The poster featured the name and possibly a picture, or at least a description, of the wanted fugitive and a price for their capture. Well, each of us has a wanted poster, with our picture and

name on it, in hell. But it doesn't read Dead or Alive—it just reads DEAD. And the price? Your soul. "Bounty hunter" demons have been assigned by Satan to track you down and bring your soul to hell by any means possible. But there is a corresponding poster in heaven as well, which reads ALIVE. God has assigned angels to guard our souls and work with the Holy Spirit to ensure that we come back to Him in heaven. Because His love for us is so great, and He created each of us to be with Him forever, He does everything possible to influence us to make the right choice.

Genesis 3:8 tells us that God would walk with Adam and Eve in the Garden of Eden and talk with them: "And they heard the sound of the Lord God walking in the garden in the cool of the day." He allowed Adam to name all the animals. He had seen Adam's loneliness and was moved to create a mate for him. We don't know how long it was after creation that Adam and Eve sinned, but it could have been many years, and they walked and talked with God all that time. When Adam and Eve did finally sin against Him, He already had a plan ready to restore the relationship and redeem man from eternal damnation.

Think about Adam and Eve for a second. They walked with God on a daily basis, were friends with all the animals, and lived in a garden of perfection where they never had to toil for their food, just care for the garden and the animals. Then one day Satan entered a serpent, and he came and tempted Eve, who in turn tempted Adam. They succumbed to sin and were thrown out of the garden, now at enmity with the animals they had been friends with the day before. They cowered in whatever shelter they could find and realized that they were now prey, instead of master, to some of the animals.

But God never abandoned them or their offspring. While He could no longer walk on earth with them, He still communicated with and looked after them. He asked for sacrifice from Cain and Abel. When He rejected Cain's offering, and Cain killed Abel, He took pity on Cain and put a mark on him so no one would kill him.

But if we really want to look at God as love, we need only to look to Jesus. He said to His disciples,

"Have I been with you so long. and yet you have not known me, Phillip? He who has seen Me has seen the Father; so how can you say, 'Show us the Father'? Do you not believe that I am in the Father, and the Father in Me? The words I speak to you I do not speak on my own authority; but My Father who dwells in Me does the work" (Jn. 14:9–10).

If we look at Jesus's ministry and life on earth, we will see God's character and know better who He is. What did Jesus do to show that God is love?

First, He had compassion on the people. Everyone who was brought to Him or even just asked, and many that He sought out, were healed. He drove out demons and set people free from their enslavement by Satan. He restored the dead to their families by raising them from death. He wept over His friend Lazarus' death, but then brought him back to life. He fed 5,000 people and their families with five small fish and two barley loaves because they were hungry. He stood up to and challenged the religious leaders, whom He accused of laying heavy burdens on the people in the name of religion to gain prestige and money. He wept over Jerusalem, knowing that the Holy City would be destroyed and the people persecuted. And He always instructed the people in God's ways to lead them to the Father and heaven—not by laying all kinds of rules on them but by telling them how to be like God in their behavior.

Then Jesus showed the ultimate act of love by submitting to death on an instrument of extreme torture to pay for our sins and to open the gates of heaven once more for us. And Jesus's reward was to be raised from the dead on the third day by His Father so He could rule forever with the Father and the Holy Spirit as God in heaven. Satan has convinced many to put down or try to discredit the story of Jesus's death and resurrection, but without it we would all be on the road to hell with no hope for eternity. Jesus was and is God's only plan of salvation for mankind and shows His unlimited love for His people.

How do we know that Jesus is the one? Let's look at the Bible.

The Messiah or Savior was first promised in Genesis 3:15 when God told Satan: "And I will put enmity between you and the woman.

.nd between your seed and her seed; He shall bruise your head, and you shall bruise His heel." In Isaiah 53. the Messiah is described as the man of sorrows:

> He is a Man of sorrows and acquainted with grief. And we hid, as it were, our face from Him; He was despised and we did not esteem Him. Surely He has born our griefs and carried our sorrows; yet we esteem Him stricken, smitten by God, and afflicted. But He was wounded for our transgressions, He was bruised for our iniquities; and by His stripes we are healed.

("Stripes" refers to marks of the lash—Jesus was whipped mercilessly by the Roman soldiers.) Satan bruised Jesus's heel by arousing the crowd at Pilate's trial of Jesus to crucify Him. Jesus bruised Satan's head by opening heaven to us and taking away his power over people.

In John 1:29–34, when John the Baptist first spotted Jesus as He approached, he said:

> "Behold! The Lamb of God who takes away the sin of the world. This is Him of whom I said, 'after me comes a Man who is preferred before me.' I did not know Him, but that He should be revealed to Israel, therefore I came baptizing with water." And John bore witness saying, "I saw the Spirit descending from heaven like a dove, and He remained upon Him. "I did not know Him, but He who sent me to baptize with water [God] said to me, 'Upon whom you see the Spirit descending, and remaining on Him, this is He who baptizes with the Holy Spirit.' And I have seen and testified that this is the Son of God." [Note: the singular *sin* is used as opposed to the plural sins of individuals. This means He took all sin from everyone.]

Jesus is referred to as the Passover Lamb. In Exodus 12, we read that a lamb was to be slaughtered and the blood sprinkled on the wooden doorposts to ward off the Angel of Death as it passed through Egypt strike down the firstborn of Egypt. Jesus was slaughtered at Passover and His blood soaked the wooden cross.

In Revelation 5:11–12, the same John who wrote the Gospel tells us that Jesus is the Lamb of God.

> Then I looked and I heard the voice of many angels around the throne, the living creatures, and the elders; and the number of them was ten thousand times ten thousand, and thousands of thousands, saying with a loud voice: "Worthy is the lamb that was slain to receive power and riches and wisdom, and strength and honor and glory and blessing!

And Revelation 5:9, "For you were slain, and have redeemed us to God by Your blood."

If John the Baptist, John the Evangelist, the angels, elders, and living creatures around the throne in heaven all tell us that Jesus is the one, we have to look no further,

6. **God is sovereign.** *Sovereign* means supreme in authority without external influence. He answers to no one but Himself. What does that mean for you? Two things come to mind.

First, God gave us free will. He does not pull strings to get us to do what He wants. He took a chance at Creation to allow people to love Him back or reject Him by giving us that choice. He could have created puppets who do His bidding all the time. But what kind of love does someone under control all the time really have? No. He wanted free individuals who would love Him back, freely. That's the chance He took. When Satan entered the pictured and Adam sinned, we stopped loving Him the way He desired. But He's still in control and has rectified the problem through Jesus.

Second, He is bound to His Word. His word is His bond. He cannot tell a lie or go back on His word. Jesus said in Matthew 16:19, "And I will give you the keys of the kingdom of heaven, and whatever you bind earth will be bound in heaven; and whatever you loose on earth will be loosed in heaven". What does that mean to you? That means that the moment you acknowledge your sins, repent of them, and confess them to God, you are forgiven. Even if He didn't love you so much and revel in your company, when you come before Him seeking forgiveness and His righteousness, He would have to forgive you anyway because He said He would. Think of that! You have only to believe in Jesus as His way of salvation, confess your sins, repent of them, and accept His forgiveness to be on the way to heaven. No matter what you've done! The only thing that can't be forgiven is not asking for it. Not believing in Jesus and accepting forgiveness and salvation is a sure ticket to hell.

After a horrible school shooting in Florida, a major news network interviewed a young male survivor. He questioned how a loving God could permit something like this to happen. He said he couldn't serve a God like that. He's dead wrong! That is the only kind of God we want to serve. Why? Because as much as it pains God, and as much He would like to stop incidents like these, He gave His word not to interfere with people's free will. He sends messengers to people to try to turn them to Him and away from evil, but if people don't listen or don't want to be turned, He can't interfere.

Unfortunately, when Jesus left the earth and ascended into heaven, He had to leave the world in the hands of people to carry on His work. We all know that some people can be real crap heads and mistreat others. The result of this mistreatment can be mental problems, and we see the disasters this causes daily. But God is still sovereign, and only turning to Him can make things right.

CHAPTER

WHAT IS HELL?

Merriam-Webster online defines hell as: the nether realm of the devil and the demons in which condemned people suffer everlasting punishment - often used in curses // go to hell. Many people mistakenly believe that hell is going to be a party place. They figure that they will pop a Bud with their friends in a constant party. Maybe they'll find a willing guy or gal and "hook up." Nothing could be farther from the truth. Hell will be a place where all your senses work, and all your moments and decisions on earth will be memories that you will regret forever as you realize the terrible mistake you've made.

Picture yourself strapped hands and feet to an oven rack in a thousand-degree oven. Your body has been changed to an everlasting body so it doesn't burn up. It also doesn't sweat, so you have no cooling whatever. You just lie there in torment with unbearable heat and searing tongues of flame engulfing your body. You're in hell. You're in total darkness owing to the absence of God. You can't see your friends, but you'll recognize their voices as they scream in terror at the torture ıd torment. But cheer up! You're not alone, and that's not all that's happening to you. There are gross things like slimy bugs, mice, rats and the like crawling all over you, biting, scratching, defecating, and urinating all over you. The urine and feces will bake to you, and the stench will be horrific. But they're not bugs or rats—they're demons, followers of Satan, and you're in their house so they get to do whatever they like to you.

But that's not the worst of it. As these "things" are tormenting and torturing you, they're also taunting you: "You could have been happy with God in heaven forever, but you chose to come down here and be with us. Why?" And they'll repeat it every moment of every day forever. And the more it bugs you, the more they'll taunt you by saying it over and over and over again. What will you answer them? You better think of your answer now, because you might be in too much pain to come up with an answer then!

Maybe that's not exactly what hell will be. Dante's *Inferno* describes it differently. Some believe it might be like molten lava. Revelation 19:20 tells us that "these two [the beast and the false prophet] were cast alive into the lake of fire burning with brimstone." You can drown in a lake. But you would never die—just go through the experience, possibly over and over and over again. You could try to get out of it. You decide to go east. You swim for a thousand years and are still not out. Then you decide to go north. You swim for a million years and are still not out. You can never get out once you're there.

Either way, it is definitely a place of torment. In Luke 16:19–31, Jesus tells the story of the rich man and Lazarus.

> "There was a certain rich man who was clothed in purple and fine linen and fared sumptuously every day. But there was a certain beggar named Lazarus, full of sores, who was laid at his gate, desiring to be fed with the crumbs which fell from the rich man's table. Moreover, the dogs came and licked his sores. So it was that the beggar died and was carried by the angels to Abraham's bosom. The rich man also died and was buried. And being in torments in Hades, he lifted up

his eyes and saw Abraham afar off, and Lazarus in his
bosom. Then he cried and said, 'Father Abraham, have
mercy on me, and send Lazarus that he may dip the
tip of his finger in water and cool my tongue, for I am
tormented in this flame.'"

Why didn't he ask for a glass or a pitcher of water? Because his
torment was so great that just the tip of a finger dipped in water would
bring some relief. Sound like a party place? Resuming at verse 25:

"But Abraham said, 'Son, remember that in your
lifetime you received your good things, and likewise
Lazarus evil things. And besides all this, between us and
you there is a great gulf fixed, so that those who want
to pass from here to you cannot, nor can those from
there pass to us.' Then he said, 'I beg you therefore,
father, that you would send him to my father's house.
For I have five brothers, that he may testify to them,
lest they also come to this place of torment.' Abraham
said to him, 'They have Moses and the prophets, let
them hear them.' And he said, 'No father Abraham, but
if one goes to them from the dead, they will repent.'
But he said to him, 'If they do not hear Moses and the
prophets, neither will they be persuaded though one
rise from the dead.'"

I hope this sounds familiar. People still don't believe today, even
though Jesus rose from the dead some two thousand years ago.

Remember September 11, 2001? The horrific events in New York,
Washington, and Pennsylvania? It's called 9/11 for short. Television
news crews filming the twin towers caught people jumping out of
the buildings. They were jumping out of windows as high up as the
seventieth to the hundredth floors. That meant a minimum fall of 700
to 1,000 feet, ending in unsurvivable contact with the ground below.
Why would rational people jump, knowing they couldn't survive?
Because they feared the fire more than the fall. They didn't want to be

urned alive in a fire. If fire caused so much panic on 9/11, why would you condemn yourself to it forever?

How bad do you have to be to go to hell? You don't have to be bad at all! Many people automatically assume that someone like Hitler or Stalin or serial killers are the kind of people who go to hell. The truth is that many good people go to hell every day, because they thought that being good would get them to heaven. They never took the time nor thought it necessary to embrace Jesus and God's plan of salvation. Not even Mother Teresa could get into heaven without her belief in Jesus.

Oh! I almost forgot. While you're suffering this terror from the torture and torments of hell, your loved ones are enjoying the perfect presence of God and perfect happiness and joy in heaven. And because heaven is perfect happiness, any memory of you or your existence has been erased from their thoughts. You see, if they thought about you and the fact that you chose not to come to heaven to be with them, it would make them sad and unhappy. Those things are not permitted in heaven. It would spoil their joy of heaven. So all memory of you has been erased from them. You may think of them and wish they could ask God to pardon you, but it's too late. God will ignore your calls and they don't remember your existence, so you suffer alone and forgotten forever.

People often describe a horrific experience as "hell on earth." There can never be hell on earth. As long as a person is on the earth, there is the opportunity to meet God and establish a relationship with Him and to accept His plan of salvation in Jesus. Once you leave the earth, hell is the complete absence of God forever. Never again can you contact God and gain what He freely offers you for all eternity. You will have blown it.

CHAPTER

4

THE TEN COMMANDMENTS

People misinterpret the purpose of the Ten Commandments and believe God is against fun and that hell is going to be the party place. Nothing could be further from the truth. After all, Jesus ate, drank, and partied (the wedding at Cana was probably a seven-day feast) with His disciples. And hell is a place of torture and torment meant for Satan and the demons who followed him from heaven, never meant for people.

The Ten Commandments are not just a checklist of dos and don'ts that God uses to determine whether we can go to heaven. The primary purpose of the Ten Commandments is to guide us in a loving response to God and His love. When we love somebody, we honor and cherish that person and want to please them. Keeping the commandments shows God that we care enough to listen and obey Him. The secondary purpose is to prevent the emptiness and pain people cause one another when our actions are contrary to these commandments.

Let's look at the commandments and see what the areas of emptiness and pain God is trying to prevent.

1. *I Am the Lord your God, who brought you out of the land of Egypt, out of the house of bondage. You shall have no other gods before me.*

Man was created to be a social being. God walked with Adam and Eve in the Garden of Eden. When man sinned, the first thing they did was hide from God because they knew they had broken God's only commandment for them not to eat of the tree. But man lost God's presence and was lonely for it. In his desperation for God, man started looking at animals or birds as his gods (idols, as for a small *g* god) and carved or molded things in wood, stone, or metal to worship them. But calling such things "gods" doesn't give them supernatural powers, and they could not fill the void sin has caused in man's heart. God knows only He can fill that void. Today we don't worship statues and carved images, but we still try to fill the void with idols like money, sex, power, and possessions. But they don't really fill the void, and when we have what we thought we craved, we still are empty and want more. People are lonely and empty, and most of our mistreatment of one another comes from this loneliness for God.

Only God can fill the void, but the US Supreme Court has decided that God has to be kept separate from government. Much of the world believes He has no place in their country. But nature abhors a vacuum, so when God is thrown out, the devil from hell and his evil move in. Terrorism, gun violence, school shootings, human trafficking, racism, riots, abortions, and the like have become the norm for the world, and sadly for streets of the United States. Many think all the problems will be fixed with more laws, like gun control or anti-hate laws with stiffer penalties. But these are not the answer. You can legislate actions, but you can't legislate morality or what is in people's hearts. We need to get God back into our daily lives and the life of the country.

The other side of the coin is being careful of your concept of God. Recently, a homosexual TV personality complained that Christians and their beliefs hurt his feelings, because "his god" would never judge him. He has created his own god to condone his sin. This is a false god and violates the second part of the commandment, and is a sure ticket to hell. Jesus showed us who God is, as recorded in the Bible, and that is the only God we should worship.

2. *You shall not take the name of the Lord your God in vain, for the Lord will not hold him guiltless who takes His name in vain.*

God told Moses in Exodus 3:14 that the people were to call Him: "I AM WHO I AM." And in Exodus 3:15 He says: "This is My name forever, and this is My memorial to all generations." Since this is His name and a memorial to all generations, it should not be used lightly or taken in vain. That means it should not be a swear word or used except in prayer.

There is power in the name of Jesus. In Acts 3:1–8, the story is told of Peter and John going to the temple and using the name of Jesus to cure a cripple.

> Now Peter and John went up together to the temple at the hour of prayer, the ninth hour. And a certain man lame from his mother's womb was carried, whom they laid daily at the gate of the temple which is called Beautiful, to ask alms from those who entered the temple; who seeing Peter and John about to go into the temple, asked for alms. And fixing his eyes on him, with John, Peter said, "Look at us." So he gave them his attention, expecting to receive something from them. Then Peter said, "Silver and gold I do not have, but what I do have I give you: In **the name** of Jesus Christ of Nazareth, rise up and walk." And he took him by the right hand and lifted him up, and immediately his feet and ankles received strength. So he, leaping up, stood and walked and entered the temple with them— walking, leaping, and praising God. (bold emphasis mine)

The Gospel of Luke tells us:

> After these things the Lord appointed seventy others also, and sent them two by two before His face into every city and place where He Himself was about to go.
>
> Then the seventy returned with joy, saying, "Lord, even the demons are subject to us in **your name**." (Luke 10:1, 17) (bold emphasis mine)

For two thousand years, people have been saved and healed by the name of Jesus. Don't abuse it. The commandment itself tells us what happens to people who misuse God's name.

3. *Remember the Sabbath day, to keep it holy.*

According to Genesis, God rested from creation on the seventh day. He didn't do it because He was tired out, but to be an example to us. He wants us to do the same, for both spiritual and physical reasons. Spiritually, He wants us to take a day and devote it to remembering Him and being in contact with Him because He loves us and wants our attention. This weekly rest reestablishes the relationship with God lost in the Garden of Eden, so important to our mental well-being.

Physically, if we work all the time, we get burned out, and we suffer both physically and mentally. God knew this would happen if we were left to our own devices, as is evidenced throughout history by workaholics, sweat shops, child labor, and alarming divorce rates caused by neglecting a spouse out of devotion to a job. He gave the command that we are to rest from work one day a week.

4. *Honor your father and your mother, that your days may be long upon the land which the Lord is giving you.*

This is the only commandment that contains a promise. If you honor your father and mother, you will have a long life and prosper in God's blessings. While many parents use this commandment to try to get young children to obey, it also applies to older adult children. While it's rare today in our society to have many generations under the same roof, His command is to look after and care for our parents as they age.

Not all parents fulfill their responsibility to bring up their children properly, and families are often torn apart by outside influences. But that does not eliminate His command to obey our parents and to see to our parents in their old age and need.

Likewise, many parents probably don't realize or think about the fact that they will be held accountable for the souls of their children. They are a gift from God, and He expects them to return to Him when they leave the earth. While each person has to make their own choice, parents are expected to educate their children about God to give them the best chance to make the right choice and return to Him when they leave this earth. This is an awesome responsibility and should not be taken lightly.

5. *You shall not murder.*

God is the author of life. Our souls are a part of His Divine Life. Since He breathes this life into us at conception and has a plan for each of our lives here on earth, only He has the right to bring that life back to Him through death. Murder deprives the person killed of their right to fulfill God's purpose for their life and attain eternal happiness. Murder rates have soared in large cities and are climbing in the suburbs. People who kill don't think about the consequences to their soul. But murderers are playing God, and that is a direct violation of the first commandment with severe consequences.

Since man is a social being, and families are bonded in love, great pain and suffering are caused when someone is killed by another. Roe s. Wade made abortion the law of the land in 1973. Since then, over 62 million unborn babies have been murdered in the abortion mills. The court justified this because medical-scientists said it's not human until it is viable, meaning it can live outside the womb. King David said in Psalm 139:13-14;

> For you formed my inmost parts; You covered me in
> my mother's womb. I will praise you, for I am fearfully

and wonderfully made; Marvelous are your works, And that my soul knows very well.

Three to four hundred years later, God confirmed what David said. In Isaiah 44:2, "Thus says the Lord who made you And formed you in the womb, who will help you..." and in verse 24, "Thus says the Lord, your Redeemer, And He who formed you from the womb: I am the Lord who makes all things..." and again in Jeremiah 1:5; "Before I formed you in the womb I knew you; Before you were born I sanctified you; I ordained you a prophet to the nations."

If God says He knows the baby in its mother's womb before it is born, then how can we say it's not human and continue to murder these babies? The US Constitution guarantees the right to life, so how can we deny the unborn that right? In Genesis 4:10, God said to Cain after he had murdered Abel, "And He said, 'What have you done? The voice of your brother's blood cries out to Me from the ground.'" How loud does the blood of 62 million murdered babies cry out to God for justice?

6. *You shall not commit adultery.*

When God created man, "Then God said, 'Let Us create man in Our image, according to Our likeness'" (Gen. 1:26). Since there is one God but three divine persons in that one God, marriage between a man and a woman, united in God, is that image of God on earth. That makes marriage a very sacred obligation. That is why Jesus said in Mark 10:9: "Therefore what God has joined together, let no man separate." When He said in Genesis 2:24, "Therefore a man shall leave his father and mother and be joined to his wife, and the two shall become one flesh," He meant they are joined—man, woman, and God—as the persons of the Trinity are joined and should not be torn apart.

But marriage is the union of two completely different personalities trying to live together in harmony. It requires work on the part of both people to make it successful. The bond of love created is fragile and easily broken by wrong words or actions. The development of the bond requires both parties to be able to open themselves up and be vulnerable to the other partner. This requires trusting the other partner and acting in a trustworthy manner.

The act of making love, or having sex, also requires complete trust, owing to the vulnerability of exposing one's self physically, emotionally, and psychologically and being completely open to your partner. This is only possible if you can trust your partner. The marriage vows call for the forsaking of all except your partner in the matter of sex. Adultery, or sex with a person you are not married to, is a breaking of that vow and does great damage to the relationship by destroying the marriage trust. The doubts and hurt created often cannot be healed and can lead to a breakup of the marriage. The result is the pain God was trying to prevent—pain for the wronged spouse, and for children who are caught in the breakup and often torn between parents. The emotional damage is serious for both groups and sometimes never really heals. This can cause a person to turn on God and they lose their relationship with Him. God did not create sex as a sport; He created it to help build the bond between a husband and wife in marriage.

The depravity of our generation is clearly demonstrated by the violation of this commandment: things such as Sex Island, where people go strictly for the purpose of having sex with as many partners as wanted; clubs that use email to bring people together for extramarital affairs; or sex trafficking, which involves kidnapping and enslaving someone so they can be sold to someone to have sex with. Imagine the pain of being kept and used this way against your will, all for someone else's few moments of "fun" and so someone can make money!

The Levitical laws, in chapter 18, tells us that we are not to uncover the nakedness of a woman or man other than our wife or husband. Yet men and women pose naked for photograrhs and act in films with sex acts in them. Pornography! Men and boys, and sadly now even women, spend hours on the internet or in sex shops devouring this material and feeding cravings. The addiction to this material leaves one unsatisfied and can foster crimes against women and children. It has been found through many studies that addiction to pornography changes a person's mind and leads to problems, including being oversexed or retreating from one's spouse—either way, creating marital problems. Jesus said if you look at a woman or man with lust in your heart, you have already committed adultery with them.

7. *You shall not steal.*

People work hard for money to buy the things they need to survive and enjoy life. When someone steals what they have worked hard for, it causes problems of how to replace the stolen goods or having to do without. Raising the money to replace these goods may be next to impossible, depending on income level and what was taken. Carjacking, home invasion robberies, and burglaries are a few of the signs of a society that no longer respects the rights of people to private property. Certain groups feel entitled to what other people have, but they lack the discipline to work and wait for the chance to purchase them legally. Wanting something so badly that you have to steal it can make it into a false god, or idol, violating the first commandment—and costing you your soul.

8. *You shall not bear false witness.*

Most people assume this commandment means not telling lies. And while this is true, because lying about things gives false impressions, it is not the only meaning of the commandment. Character assassination, which can destroy a person's good name and reputation, is also forbidden. Politicians especially seem to have forgotten this commandment.

We live in a post–truth generation, where anything I feel, or believe is truth, becomes *my* truth. The absolute truth of God's word is ignored, or worse yet attacked as "hate speech," because it doesn't line up with the liberal agenda. The reality is that God's Word is not hate, but love.

9. *You shall not covet (envy or desire) your neighbor's goods.*

God gives to each of us what we need and what He knows will be good for our relationship with Him. When we are envious or jealous of what we have, compared to what someone else has, we are telling Him that we know better than He does what we need. Often, it isn't *needing* a thing so much as just desiring to have it. If left unchecked, this desire can injure or destroy our trust in God and lead us to do something like stealing, which in turn causes loss of our relationship with God and pain to the person we stole from. If you truly desire something you don't have, ask God for it. If it is good for you, He will give it to you, in His time. The devil uses advertising to make us want things that God knows will do us harm. Be careful not to succumb to these desires. Ask God!

10. You shall not covet (envy or desire) your neighbor's wife.

This commandment applies to all men and woman, whether married or not. As we explained in the sixth commandment, the sexual relationship was created by God to be used in marriage only. The marriage vows call for forsaking all others emotionally and sexually. Whether we are single or married to someone whom we are not totally satisfied with, we are not to look to another man or woman for that satisfaction. Self-preservation or preserving one's life is the strongest drive in living beings. Self-propagation, or keeping the species going, is the second. That means that in humans, sex is a very powerful drive. Left unfulfilled, it can create problems for both men and women. Pornography, whether it's photographs, films, or videos, intensify these desires and can lead to crimes against another person. Looking to another person to fulfill a lacking marriage only leads to disaster. Counseling should be the first avenue to resolve any issues, not committing adultery.

CHAPTER

THE US CONSTITUTION

The US Constitution was written 245 years ago by men. The Word of God was written into men's hearts at creation. The Supreme Court has made several decisions recently that have gone against God's Word and the Ten Commandments, and as such are wrong. Their attempt to be "politically correct" and "inclusive" has led them to interpret the Constitution incorrectly. They have also usurped the domain of Congress in making their decisions the law of the land. The Constitution is quite clear about the separation of powers in the three distinct branches of the government. Lawmaking is not the purview of the Supreme Court. That function is reserved exclusively for Congress.

Those distinctions have been run over by the current Supreme Court. It's time to get back to the constitution as it was written. The Supreme Court hears individual cases and decides on their merits only. The states, through the people, decide what will be the laws of that state and thus the law of the land.

Let's look at four areas in which the Supreme Court has ruled against God's word.

1. **Abortion.** Liberals argued that the right to equal access guaranteed by the Constitution guarantees the right to abortion. The Constitution, first and foremost guarantees the right to life. Medical scientists argued that the embryo, or fetus, is not human unless it can live outside the womb or be what they call "viable." As we explored above, God knitted us together in our mother's womb and knew us before we were born. We are human from the moment of conception. He also gave the commandment "Thou shall not kill." Abortion is murder. Partial birth abortion is infanticide. Roe v. Wade, the decision legalizing abortion nationwide, was based on false premises.

Sixty-two million babies have been murdered since Roe, and the blood of those babies cries out to God for vengeance. The Bible tells us that God hates those whose hands shed innocent blood. The hands of those who perform or assist with abortions, or those who have abortions, are covered in the blood of those innocent children. They must confess their sin and repent, or they will lose their souls.

2. **Separation of church and state.** The constitution was written by God-fearing men who believed that Biblical principles were the only way to ensure that freedom would be maintained in this country. The phrase "separation of church and state" comes from a letter Thomas Jefferson wrote to a Southern Baptist church assuring them of freedom to practice their religion without government interference. Humanists, however, have denied God and His Word and the fact that the Constitution was written around Biblical principles. Our society today has believed them, turned their backs on God, and adopted this philosophy. The phrase was turned against religion and used to throw God out of schools and government. That means decisions are made are based on godless humanism or worse, atheism. All the Constitution really says on the subject is the there will be no state-established church, which is what the early

settlers from Europe were trying to escape. This in no way implies throwing God out of everything.

The First Amendment in the Bill of Rights guarantees the right to the free and unencumbered practice of religion. That means no government interference or restrictions. The federal government and the IRS have used tax status as a weapon to restrict what may or may not be said in churches. This is the government interference strictly forbidden by the constitution. It also restricts the message the churches need to deliver and has watered down the message of salvation. How many people would make the right choice if the message delivered was what it was meant to be?

As I write, Congress is considering the Equality Act, which threatens religious freedom. Institutions and businesses will be forced to hire people who do not share their beliefs or be threatened with loss of license and the right to stay in business if they don't comply. The Equality Act does just the opposite of what it says and promotes inequality. It discriminates against anyone who does not hold to far-left liberal views, and limits the free practice of religion in violation of the Constitution.

3. **Gay rights.** The Supreme Court has ruled that the constitutional guarantee of equal access also justifies "gay rights," including same-sex marriage. While one can rightfully argue that all people have the same rights under the Constitution and discrimination is wrong, there can be no such thing as "gay marriage." Man did not institute marriage; God did. In Genesis 2:24, He said: "Therefore a **man** shall leave his father and mother and be joined to his **wife** and they shall become one flesh" (emphasis mine). A man is the husband as defined by God, and a woman is the wife as defined by God.

Not only that, but Leviticus 18:22 tells us, "You shall not lie with a male as with a woman. It is an abomination." And again: "If a man lies with a male as he lies with a woman, both of them have committed an abomination. They shall surely be put to death. Their blood shall be upon them" (Leviticus 20:13). Therefore, there can be no such thing as "gay" or "same-sex" marriage, since it takes one of each sex to make a true marriage in God's eyes. That does not mean that homosexuals and lesbian cannot be loved, accepted, and welcomed into God's church family. But the welcoming church must inform them of the error of their ways and work to bring about a change of lifestyle. The church cannot be construed as condoning the lifestyle. If this offends the person and they refuse to change or abstain from the practice, then they should not continue in the church.

God gave mankind the rainbow as a sign of His covenant not to destroy the whole world ever again by flood:

> "I set my rainbow in the cloud, and it shall be a sign of the covenant between Me and the earth. It shall be, when I bring a cloud over the earth, that the rainbow shall be seen in the cloud; and I will remember My covenant which is between Me and you and every living creature of all flesh; the waters shall never again become a flood to destroy all flesh. The rainbow shall be in the cloud, and I will look on it to remember the everlasting covenant between God and every living creature of all flesh on the earth." And God said to Noah, "This is the sign of the covenant which I have established between Me and all flesh that is on the earth." (Gen. 9:13–17)

Now the LGBTQ community has mocked God by taking the sign of His covenant, the rainbow, and making it their flag as a symbol of their sin, flaunting themselves in His face with their gay pride month and parades.

If the LGBTQ community really believes that God should change His mind and conform to them because society has changed its morals and calls their immorality an "alternate lifestyle," they have only to look at the biblical story of Sodom and Gomorrah to see what their outcome will be.

> Now two angels came to Sodom in the evening, and Lot was sitting in the gate of Sodom. When Lot saw

them, he rose to meet them, and bowed with his face toward the ground. And he said, "Here now my lords, please turn in to your servant's house and spend the night, and wash your feet; then you may rise early and go on your way." And they said, "No, but we will spend the night in the open square." But he insisted strongly; so they turned into him and entered his house. Then he made them a feast, and baked unleavened bread, and they ate. Now before they lay down, the men of the city, the men of Sodom, both old and young, all the people from every quarter, surrounded the house. And they called to Lot and said to him, "Where are the men who came to you tonight? Bring them out to us that we may know them both carnally." So Lot went out to them through the doorway, shut the door behind him, and said, "Please, my brethren, do not do so wickedly! See now, I have two daughters who have not known a man; please let me bring them out to you, and you may do to them as you wish: only do nothing to these men, since this is the reason they have come under the shadow of my roof." (Gen. 19:1–8)

The law of hospitality was an important law during this time. Someone who entered your home was under your protection. Lot was trying to protect the angels from the townsmen who wanted to have sex with the angels against their will. That's what prompted Lot to offer his daughters in exchange for the angels.

And they said, "Stand back!" Then they said, "This one came in to stay here, and he keeps acting as a judge; now we will deal worse with you than with them." So they pressed hard against the man Lot, and came near to break down the door. But the men [the angels] reached out their hands and pulled Lot into the house with them, and shut the door. And they struck the men who were at the doorway of the house with blindness, both small and great, so that they became weary trying to find the door. Then the men said to Lot, "Have you anyone else here? Son-in-law, your sons, your daughters, and whomever you have in the city—take them out of this place! For we will destroy this place, because the outcry against them has grown great before the face of the Lord, and the Lord has sent us to destroy it.".... When the morning dawned, the angels urged Lot to hurry, saying, "Arise, take your wife and your two daughters who are here, lest you be consumed in the punishment of the city." ... So it came to pass, when they had brought them outside, that he said. "Escape for your life! Do not look behind you nor stay anywhere in the plain. Escape to the mountains, lest you be destroyed." ... Then the Lord rained brimstone and fire on Sodom and Gomorrah, from the Lord out of the heavens. So He overthrew those cities, all the plain, and all the inhabitants of the cities, and what grew on the ground. (Gen. 19:9–13, 15, 17, 24–25)

Those who question the Bible and think these are just stories should look at Explorers Web October 6, 2021. Archeologists from Veritas International University, and Trinity Southwest University have discovered what they believe is the city of Sodom in a dig at Tell el-Hammam, in the plains by the Dead Sea. They have determined that it was destroyed from above by an air blast from something like a meteorite, resulting in fire and brimstone. The archeologists speculated that God sent a meteorite to destroy the city.

4. **Gender Identity.** There can be no question of gender identity: "So God created man in His own image; in the image of God he created him; male and female He created them" (Gen. 1:27). There are only two genders, male and female. Anything else is a lie of the devil. People promoting or taking part in altering gender, especially with little children, are playing God and telling Him that He made

a mistake and that they know better than He does what gender they should be. God never makes mistakes!

Jesus was very clear in three gospels about scandalizing others. when He said: Luke 17:1-2, "It is impossible that no offense should come, but woe to him through whom they do come! It would be better for him if a millstone was hung around his neck, and he were thrown into the sea, than that he should offend one of these little ones." Mark 9:42, "But whoever causes one these little ones who believe in Me to stumble, it would be better for him if a millstone were hung around his neck and he were thrown into the sea." Matthew 18:6, "But whoever causes one of these little ones who believe in me to sin, it would be better for him if a millstone were hung around his neck and he were drowned in the depths of the sea.

Anyone who preaches abortion, same-sex sex, same-sex marriage, or gender transition is giving scandal to those who listen to them and are causing them to sin. They are exercising their choice to go to hell.

CHAPTER

ANTI-SEMITISM: THE WAR AGAINST THE JEWISH PEOPLE

You're probably wondering why a topic like anti-Semitism is in a book on choosing to go to hell. Anti-Semitism is anti-God. You can't hate the Jewish people and love God. The Jewish people are God's chosen people. And if you don't love God, you won't get into heaven. That leaves only one destination for your soul.

Two-State Solution

The United Nations has been telling the world the lie that the Jewish people are occupying the land of Israel. Abdulia Shahid, President of the Assembly, said in the General assembly meeting of December 1, 2021: "mere words are of no use to Palestinian people as they suffer decades of occupation, arbitrary arrest, and illegal settlements…"

Nothing could be further from the truth. God gave Abram, before his name was changed to Abraham, the land in perpetuity (forever):

> And the Lord said to Abram, after Lot had separated from him: "Lift your eyes now and look from the place where you are—northward, southward, eastward and westward; for all the land which you see I give to you and your descendants **forever**." (Genesis. 13:14–15) [emphasis mine]

The Jewish people are not descended from any of the people who originally occupied the land of Canaan. Those nations were idol worshippers. Abraham came from the land of Ur of the Chaldeans. He was brought by God to Canaan because he worshipped the true God and not idols. God made the way to clear the land from idol worshippers and establish the Jewish race.

The Palestinians are descendants from some of those original nations, and as such have no claim to the land of Israel or Jerusalem. Not only that, but God established Jerusalem as His dwelling place on earth forever:

> "For now I have chosen and sanctified this house [the Temple of Solomon in Jerusalem], that My name may be there forever; and My eyes and My heart will be there perpetually." (2 Chronicles 7:16)

> And he carried me away in the Spirit to a great and high mountain, and showed me the great city, the holy Jerusalem, descending out of heaven from God. (Revelation 21:10)

The United Nations, and unfortunately the present American administration, are calling for a "two-state solution" to the problems in Israel. The Bible is very clear that God gave the land of Israel to the Jewish people forever. Therefore, the only solution is for the Palestinians to join the Jewish people in Israel and live peacefully with them. The Palestinian Liberation Organization (PLO) and Hamas, the Palestinian governing body, however, have no intentions of living peacefully with the Jewish people. Their stated intentions are to liberate the Palestinian people and drive Israel out and occupy the land for themselves. God will never allow this to happen. His promise to Abraham was forever: "I will bless those who bless you, and I will curse him who curses you, and in you all the families of the earth shall be blessed" (Gen. 12:3)

Replacement Theology

Replacement theology states that the church has replaced the Jewish people as God's chosen people. Unfortunately, even the present pope espouses this philosophy. Nothing could be further from the truth. We will look at biblical proof that God still holds the Jewish people in the same regard today as He did in the days when He made the promises.

Jesus said in John 15:1-2 "I am the true vine and My Father is the vine dresser. Every branch in Me that does not bear fruit he takes away; and every branch that bears fruit He prunes, that it may bear more fruit". This analogy would have been very meaningful to the Jewish people of His time, since they were an agricultural society. He also said in Matthew 15:24 that salvation through Him was (at that time) for the Jewish people alone: "But He answered and said, 'I was not sent except to the lost sheep of the house of Israel.'" But the house of Israel did not believe or accept Him.

Romans 11:11–12 tells us about the Jewish people's unbelief:

> I say then, have they [the Jewish people] stumbled that they should fall? Certainly not! But through their fall, to provoke them to jealousy, salvation has come to the Gentiles. Now if their fall is riches for the world, and their failure riches for the Gentiles, how much more their fullness.

The gentiles were grafted into the vine of salvation. Romans 11:19–21 and 23–24 tells us that the Jewish people were cut off because they failed to believe in Jesus as the Messiah but that they will be grafted back in the end times.

You will say then, "Branches were cut off that I might be grafted in." Well said. Because of unbelief they were broken off, and you stand by faith. Do not be haughty, but fear. For if God did not spare the natural branches, He might not spare you either. ...And they [the Jewish people] also, if they do not continue in unbelief, will be grafted in, for God is able to graft them in again. For if you were cut out of the olive tree which is wild by nature, and were grafted contrary to nature into a cultivated olive tree, how much more will these [the Jewish people] who are natural branches, be grafted into their own olive tree."

To espouse or believe in replacement theology shows either ignorance of or unbelief in God's Word. In John 3:18, Jesus was very specific about failing to believe and its consequences: "He who believes in Him is not condemned; but he who does not believe is condemned already, because he has not believed in the name of the only begotten Son of God."

Boycott, Divest, and Sanctions (BDS)

BDS is a movement to cripple the nation of Israel's economy and destroy it from within by economic collapse. It is an attack on Israel just as surely as missiles, rockets, bombs, suicide bombers, and the like. Those who advocate for or take part in BDS are making war on Israel and God.

The United States is sailing in dangerous waters. President Donald Trump's administration strengthened America's relationship with Israel, moved the US embassy to Jerusalem, recognized Jerusalem as Israel's capital, and brokered the Abraham Accords with Israel's neighbors. These moves helped delay God's wrath against the US for all its transgression: abortion, gay movements, gender changes, and so on. But the present administration has weakened that support for Israel and wants to reenter the Iran Nuclear Deal. Members of "the squad in the House of Representatives blocked legislation to fund Israel's Iron Dome anti-missile system and Rep. Ilhan Omar made an anti-Semitic speech on the floor of the House in March 2019. If this nation continues in this direction, God's promise to Abraham, and as such to Israel, will come upon America: "I will curse him who curses you."

CONCLUSION

Do those who favor the Constitution over God's Word, or ignore or disbelieve His Word, really think there is going to be a copy of the Constitution on a bookstand placed between them and God when they stand before Him in judgment after they die, so they can argue the Constitution with Him? It won't do any good. God can put together a jury of more than twelve men who wrote the Constitution, and they will verify that they wrote it with the Bible as its foundation. They knew that only adherence to His Word would guarantee the success of this country. It's only this current politically correct, humanistic Supreme Court of today that interprets the Constitution against His word. And if you want to know why we have all the gun violence and school shootings today, it's because we have thrown out these principles and are living without God and His Word as our guide.

Moreover, the ancient Hebrew people petitioned Moses to beg God not to speak to them, except through Moses, because His voice was like thunder and scared the people. I wouldn't want to be in the same universe when God answers someone who starts to argue the Constitution against His word.

There is only one thing that will stand between you and God the Father when you stand before Him at the end of your life. It will be His Living Word, His Son Jesus. God the Father will open the book of your life and go through every moment of it. He will reveal everything to all: every thought you thought and shouldn't have thought, or should have thought and didn't; every word you spoke and shouldn't have spoken, or should have and didn't; and every action you took and shouldn't have taken, or should have taken and didn't. He will reveal everything to all.

Then He will close the book and look at Jesus. Jesus will turn and look at you for a time. Then He will turn back and look at His Father with one of two looks on His face.

He may have a smile on His face and inform His Father, "This is one of mine. Their name in written in the Book of Life." Whereupon God the Father will smile at you and say: "Well done, good and faithful servant. Now enter into the rest prepared you from the beginning of time." Then the angels will take you off to heaven forever.

Or, Jesus will have a sad look on His face and inform His Father, "I do not know this one. Their name is not written in the Book of Life. They rejected me on earth, so I must reject them now." Then God the Father will frown at you and say, "You worthless wretch. Depart from me into the fires of hell created for the devil and his followers." Then the demons will carry you off to hell forever.

You will cry out to God for help, thinking that this is a mistake. He could come down and pluck you out and take you to heaven with Him. He has the power. But He won't. You chose to reject Him in this world. If He came and rescued you now, that would violate your free will and negate His promise of free will to choose Him or not. So, hell is where you stay forever.

You can't escape judgment! The question is, will you accept that Jesus died on the cross for your sins, to take your place and face God's judgment for you, so that you could be acquitted and gain heaven? Or will you reject Jesus, and be judged by God apart from Jesus and be condemned?

Will you choose to accept Him and His plan of salvation through Jesus? Or will you choose not to make that choice and just allow your soul to end up in hell forever? The saddest part of this whole scenario is that the choice is strictly yours!

THE END.

No, wait! It's not the end. It's just the beginning of that which will last forever. Make the right choice. Choose God!

Printed in the United States
by Baker & Taylor Publisher Services